seeds

mel pennant

seeds was first produced by tiata fahodzi and Wrested Veil
in association with Leeds Playhouse, Soho Theatre and Tara Finney Productions,
receiving its world premiere at Leeds Playhouse on 21 February 2020.

seeds
by mel pennant

cast

evelyn	judith jacob
jackie	penny layden

creative team

director	anastasia osei-kuffour
designer	helen coyston
lighting designer	simisola majekodunmi
sound designer	xana
casting director	nadine rennie
voice coach	aundrea fudge
graphic designer	carolyne hill
photography	wasi daniju
film	cassie quarless

production team

producers	tiata fahodzi and wrested veil in association with leeds playhouse, soho theatre and tara finney productions
general manager	live general management
production manager	dan gosselin
stage manager	ami gaskin
pr	chloe nelkin consulting

supporters

This production would not have been possible without the generous support of:

thanks

We would also like to thank:
eStage Group
White Light
Stage Sound Services
Philip Carne
Tom Chapman
Lee Hunter
Ntonga Mwanza
Eleanor Turner

a note from the producers

seeds is a courageous play that looks at difficult subjects of racism,
violence, death and grief. It describes a hate crime and uses the n-word,
all of which may be a trigger for people who have suffered as result of the
above and may be difficult for some readers.

Please take care of yourselves. If you feel provoked but the content, do
reach out to someone – a family member, friend or get in touch with
a professional organisations such as Cruse Bereavement Care on 0808
808 1677 or Victims Support on 0808 168 9111.

www.cruse.org.uk
www.victimsupport.org.uk

cast

judith jacob – evelyn

Television credits include: *Dark Heart, British Rationals, Still Open All Hours, Rellik, The Five, Eastenders, Doctors, Holby City, Angels, My Family, No Problem, Provoked, Radio Roo, The Bill, The Queen's Nose* and *The Real McCoy.*

Film credits include: *No Shade, Captain Phillips* and *Respect.*

Theatre credits include: *The Interrogation Of Sandra Bland* (Bush Theatre), *Real McCoy* (Heartbeat), *An Evening With Gary Lineker* (Hornchurch), *Goldilocks* (Hackney Empire), *The Healing* (Omnibus Theatre), *Get Raunchy* – BiBi Crew (Stratford East) and *On A Level* (Stratford East).

penny layden – jackie

Theatre credits include: *Jellyfish, Macbeth, My Country: A Work in Progress, Another World: Losing Our Children to Islamic State, An Oak Tree, Everyman, Edward II, Table, Timon of Athens* (National Theatre), *The Tempest, Roberto Zucco, Measure for Measure* (RSC), *Cleft* (Rough Magic/Galway Festival), *Sketching* (Wilton's Music Hall), *The Lorax, Cinderella* (Old Vic), *Bright Phoenix* (Liverpool Everyman), *Beryl* (West Yorkshire Playhouse), *Nora* (Belgrade, Coventry), *Lidless* (Trafalgar Studios/Hightide Festival/Edinburgh), *Draw Me Close, Vernon God Little, The Art of Random Whistling* (Young Vic), *The Bacchae, Mary Barton, Electra, Mayhem* (Manchester Royal Exchange), *Dancing at Lughnasa* (Birmingham Rep), *Romeo and Juliet, The Antipodes, Hamlet* (Shakespeare's Globe), *Comfort Me With Apples* (Hampstead Theatre/Tour), *Assassins* (Sheffield Crucible), *Seasons Greetings, Popcorn* (Liverpool Playhouse), *The Laramie Project* (West End), *A Passage to India, The Magic Toyshop, Jane Eyre* (Shared Experience), *Maid Marian and her Merry Men* (Bristol Old Vic), *What I Did In The Holidays, The Plough and the Stars, Hunchback Of Notre Dame, Dangerous Corner, A Midsummer Night's Dream* (New Vic, Stoke).

Television credits include: *Belgravia, Casualty, My Country: A Work in Progress, Grantchester, Dark Angel, Prisoner's Wives, Call the Midwife, Land Girls, Sirens, South Riding, Silent Witness, Poppy Shakespeare, Bad Mother's Handbook, Waterloo Road, No Angels, Murphy's Law, Fat Friends, Outlaws.*

Film credits include: *Broken* and *The Libertine.*

creative team

mel pennant – writer

Mel Pennant is a playwright, screenwriter and novelist. She graduated from the London College of Communication in 2014 with an MA in Screenwriting.

In 2013, her play *No Rhyme* won the Brockley Jack Write Now 4 Award and was produced by the Brockley Jack Theatre for a short run. Mel has been involved with the Tamasha Theatre Company writing for the Barbican Box. She's been in a week's development programme at the Barbican with six young actors and written a short play called *Smile* in collaboration with the National Archives. *Smile* was shown at Rich Mix and was turned into a radio play. It is available online.

Mel was recently commissioned by the Belgrade Coventry Theatre and Tamasha to collaborate on a project which will be available for Coventry's City of Culture in 2021.

In 2018/2019, Mel was awarded a place on the Hachette/Tamasha pilot scheme for aspiring playwrights and novelists and is currently developing her first novel, *The Corpse on Bute Street*.

In 2017, Mel was also shortlisted for the Alfred Fagon Award for her play *A Black Fella Walks into a Bar*. The play was later reworked as *seeds*.

anastasia osei-kuffour – director

Anastasia Osei-Kuffour is a writer and director, trained through the Young Vic Directors Programme. She is currently Associate Director at Theatre503, has just completed two years as Trainee Artistic Director at tiata fahodzi as part of the Artistic Director Leadership Programme and is Artistic Director of Wrested Veil theatre company.

Direction includes: *Typical* (Pleasance Courtyard Edinburgh Fringe & Soho Theatre); *Cuttin' It* (Royal Court, UK schools tour); *Footprints on the Moon* (Finborough Theatre); *An Adventure* (an excerpt, Bush Theatre); *Cell* (Young Vic); *Here Comes the Bride* (Black Lives, Black Words at Bush Theatre); *All the Ways to Say Goodbye* (Young Vic); *Hosea's Girl* (Talawa Studio Firsts); *Dishonour*, *You Know That I'll Be Back*, *Universally Speaking* (Theatre503); *Pushers* (Etcetera).

Associate and Assistant Director credits include: *good dog* (UK Tour); *mixed brain* (Roundabout, Summer Hall Edinburgh); *Macbeth*, *Romeo and Juliet* (National Theatre Dorfman, Stratford Circus, UK schools tour); *Cuttin' It* – Young Vic's Jerwood Assistant Director Programme, supported by the Jerwood Charitable Foundation (Young Vic, Royal Court, Birmingham REP, Sheffield Theatres and The Yard); *Flowering Cherry*, *Alpha Beta*, *Andy Capp* (Finborough); *Three Generations of Women* (Greenwich); *Plaques and Tangles* (Royal Court); *Idomeneus* (Gate); *Henry the Fifth* (Unicorn); and – as Boris Karloff Trainee Assistant Director – *A Doll's House* (Young Vic).

helen coyston – designer

Theatre credits include: *Homing Birds* (Kali Theatre); *Puss in Boots* (The Theatre Chipping Norton); *Operation Mincemeat* (New Diorama Theatre); *Everything I see Swallow* (The Lowry/Summerhall); *The Art of Gaman* (Theatre503); *The Wizard of Oz* (Taunton Brewhouse); *Feed* (The Lowry/Pleasance) *Sex with Robots and Other Devices* (King's Head Theatre); *Alice in Wonderland, Stepping Out, A Christmas Carol, The 39 Steps, Build a Rocket, Goth Weekend* (Stephen Joseph Theatre); *Our Mutual Friend* (Hull Truck); *Antigone* (UK tour); *The Acedian Pirates* (Theatre503); *My Mother Said I Never Should* (St James Theatre); *Made Up Stories From My Unmade Bed* (Lyric Hammersmith/Latitude Festival); *Peter Pan, Watership Down, There is a War* (Watford Palace Theatre); *Bluebird* (Edinburgh Fringe).

simisola majekodunmi – lighting designer

Graduated from RADA with a specialist degree in Lighting Design.

Theatre credits include: *Lucid* (New Public Company); *Tiger Under the Skin* (New Public Company); *J'ouvert* (Theatre503); *Driving Miss Daisy* (York Theatre Royal); *Baby Box* (York Theatre Royal Studio).

Future works: *Invisible Harmony* (Southbank Centre); *Foxes* (Theatre503).

xana – sound designer

Xana is an Offie-nominated sound designer, live loop musician, sound artist, theatre maker and poet who has worked on critically-acclaimed theatre shows, films and performed in cities around the world. Xana's work focuses on archives and embodying our future narratives and memories through sci-fi, magical realism and blending genres orchestral noise/thick bass.

Xana features on the award-winning track *Afronaut* on the Mercury prize-nominated album *Driftglass* by Seed Ensemble. Xana is Associate Artist at Ovalhouse Theatre creating new show *Swallowing Your Idols*, co-organiser of Afrotech Fest and publishes the children's comic *Afronaut Squad*.

Theatre credits include: *Ivan and the Dogs, Fairview* (Young Vic); *Strange Fruit* (Bush Theatre); *Grey, Just Another Day and Night* (Ovalhouse); *Nightclubbing* (Tour); *Pink Lemonade* (Gate Theatre); *Mapping Brent Festival, Blood Knot* (Orange Tree Theatre); *SEX SEX MEN MEN* (Pecs Drag Kings/Yard Theatre); *Noughts and Crosses* (Pilot/Derby Theatre); *Burgerz* (Hackney Showroom); *Obama and Me* (Talawa); *Black Holes* (The Place); *Hive City Legacy* (Roundhouse); *Half-breed* (Soho Theatre); *Primetime* (Royal Court Theatre).

live general management – general manager

Launched in 2019, LIVE is a new company providing bespoke general management services to theatrical productions in the UK and internationally, run by Tara Finney.

Recent projects include general management of UK No.1 Tours *A Bunch of Amateurs* and *The Entertainer* (starring Shane Richie), as well as consulting on the re-brand of the Tabard Theatre to the Chiswick Playhouse and advising Wishful Thinking Musicals on their development slate. LIVE also acts as a tour booker.

dan gosselin - production manager

Graduated with a Masters degree in Engineering from Durham University in 2015.

Theatre credits include: *A Place for We* (Park Theatre); *An Unfinished Man* (Yard Theatre); *Gentlemen* (Arcola Theatre); *Cinderella: A Drag Panto* (Trafalgar Studios); *The Greatest Play in the History of the World…* (Trafalgar Studios); *Dirty Crusty* (Yard Theatre); *Disney in the West-End Summer Pop-up* (Covent Garden); *Queen of the Mist* (Brockley Jack Studio and Charing Cross Theatre); *Sh!tfaced Showtime* (Underbelly Festival Southbank); *Summer Rolls* (Park Theatre and Bristol Old Vic); *Festive Bike Ride* (Omnibus Theatre); *Salome* (Theatre N16).

Dan has also worked in the fringes as Festival Production Manager for both the Durham Drama Festival and Durham Festival of the Arts and as Deputy Head of Lighting for The Warren, part of Brighton Fringe Festival 2019.

He is a director of eStage, a collective of theatre people that works across the theatre industry to understand people's problems and deliver uniquely tailored tools, production support, and digital services that make everyone's lives easier, all whilst driving new standards in production.

ami gaskin – stage manager

Graduated from Canterbury Christ Church University with a degree in performing arts.

Theatre credits include: *The Love of the Nightingale* (The MTA); *Women, Power and Politics* (ALRA North); *Wuthering Heights* (Oxford Shakespeare Company); *The Remains of the Day* (Royal & Derngate and out of joint); *Dear Santa* (Norwell Lapley Productions Ltd); *There Was an Old Lady Who Swallowed a Fly* (The People's Theatre Company).

'...gorgeous theatre from a truly diverse company'
Lenny Henry, OBE

tiata fahodzi – a theatre company for Britain today and the Britain of tomorrow

Founded in 1997, our journey mirrors that of the British Africans we seek to serve; from early productions telling stories of emigration and diaspora (tickets and ties) to, under second artistic director Lucian Msamati, reflecting on the relationship Britain and British-Africans have with Africa (belong). In 2014 Natalie Ibu became our third Artistic Director and with her came a question: what does it mean to be of African heritage but of mixed experience? During her tenure, we continue to reflect the changing and developing diaspora with a particular interest in the dual and the in-between, in those who straddle worlds, cultures, languages, classes, heritages, races and struggles. It's in this – the messy, the multiple and the complicated identity politics – that tiata fahodzi sits, acknowledging that our audiences are more complex and contrasting than ever. Our work starts with the contemporary British African experience but reaches beyond to ask us all, what does it mean to live here, now?

staff members

artistic director and ceo	natalie ibu
finance director	kate sarley
office manager	annemarie mohan
friendship producer	kiki brown

board members
edward kemp I lucia masundire I mwiza mkandawire I sarah-jane rawlings I elouise west

patrons
lenny henry OBE I jocelyn jee esien I jenny jules I danny sapani I hugh quarshie

support us

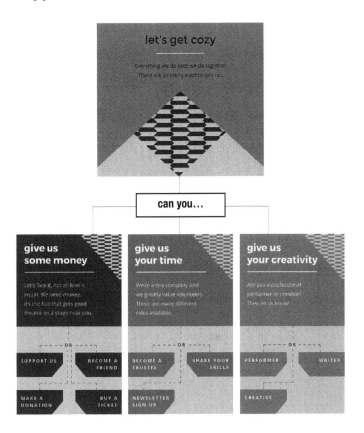

We're a tiny company with huge ambitions and to realise our aspirations we need...
a little – well, a lot – of help from our friends.

Let's get cozy, email us at **annemarie@tiatafahodzi.com**

www.tiatafahodzi.com

@tiatafahodzi
facebook.com/tiatafahodzi
instagram.com/tiatafahdozi

Supported by
**ARTS COUNCIL
ENGLAND**

WRESTED VEIL

Wrested Veil is a producing company unveiling stories with potency and flourish, founded in 2017 to produce *Footprints On The Moon* at the Finborough Theatre. It is led by writer, director and producer Anastasia Osei-Kuffour with a desire to reveal stories that explore truth and the human story behind real world issues, in the hope of sparking change.

@WrestedVeil

There has been a Playhouse in Leeds for almost 50 years; from 1970 to 1990 as Leeds Playhouse, then, with the opening of a new theatre on its current Quarry Hill site it became West Yorkshire Playhouse until reclaiming its original name in 2018.

Leeds Playhouse is one of the UK's leading producing theatres; a cultural hub, a place where people gather to tell and share stories and to engage in world class theatre. It makes work which is pioneering and relevant, seeking out the best companies and artists to create inspirational theatre in the heart of Yorkshire. From large-scale spectacle to intimate performance we develop and make work for our stages, for found spaces, for touring, for schools and community centres. We create work to entertain and inspire. As dedicated collaborators, we work regularly with other organisations from across the UK, independent producers, and some of the most distinctive, original voices in theatre today. Through our Furnace programme, we develop work with established practitioners and find, nurture and support new voices that ought to be heard. We cultivate artists by providing creative space for writers, directors, companies and individual theatre makers to refine their practice at any stage of their career. Alongside our work for the stage we are dedicated to providing creative engagement opportunities that excite and stimulate. We build, run and sustain projects which reach out to everyone from refugee communities, to young people and students, to older communities and people with learning disabilities. At the Playhouse there is always a way to get involved.

www.LeedsPlayhouse.org.uk

@LeedsPlayhouse
facebook.com/LeedsPlayhouse
instagram.com/LeedsPlayhouse

Soho Theatre is London's most vibrant theatre for new theatre, comedy and cabaret. They are a charity and social enterprise, driven by a passion for the work they produce, the artists they work with and the audiences they attract. Soho Theatre's home is in the heart of the West End - three performance spaces, a busy bar, and a fast-changing festival programme with up to six shows a night. Firmly established on the London cultural scene, they're now expanding into an additional 1,000 seat venue in Walthamstow, touring across the UK, India and Australia, and creating digital content.

www.sohotheatre.com

@sohotheatre
facebook.com/sohotheatre
instagram.com/sohotheatre

Tara Finney Productions (TFP) is an award-winning, independent theatre production company, founded in 2013 to produce *Land of Our Fathers* which was Time Out's Fringe Show of the Year. The production subsequently transferred to Trafalgar Studios in 2014 and toured England & Wales for 14 weeks in 2015/16 before returning to London's hottest pop-up theatre, Found111. The production was also filmed by Riverside Studios and released on BBC Arts Online.

Recently, TFP's 20th anniversary production of Enda Walsh's *Disco Pigs* starring Evanna Lynch transferred to the Irish Repertory Theatre, New York, garnering a Critics' Pick from the New York Times. In spring 2019, TFP's co-production with tiata fahodzi of *good dog* by Olivier Award-nominated writer Arinzé Kene completed its second tour of the UK and *Build a Rocket* was a Best Theatre Weekly Award winner at the Adelaide Fringe before touring the UK this autumn. In 2019, TFP was also associate producer on the world premiere of Oscar nominated writer Anthony McCarten's (*Bohemian Rhapsody, Darkest Hour, The Theory of Everything*) new play *The Pope* at Royal & Derngate, Northampton, which was recently turned into a film by Netflix (*The Two Popes*) which was nominated for three Oscars.

TFP's productions have been nominated for in excess of twenty-five awards including Off West End Awards, UK Theatre Awards, the Susan Smith Blackburn Award and the Chita Rivera Awards, New York.

www.tarafinney.com

@tara_finney
facebook.com/tarafinneyproductions
instagram.com/tarafinneyproducer

seeds

mel pennant

Characters

EVELYN, *mid-fifties*
JACKIE, *early fifties*

Notes on the Play

A dash (–) indicates an abrupt interruption.

… indicates a trailing off.

Dialogue in [square brackets] is intention, not to be spoken.

Any dates in the play can be changed and would ideally be adjusted to the date of the performance.

This text went to press before the end of rehearsals and so may differ slightly from the play as performed.

A living room. Modestly decorated with at least a sofa, coffee table, bookcase, and a clock. On a wall, a framed painting of MICHAEL (*black, fourteen*).

On the coffee table: birthday cake candles and a cooker lighter.

EVELYN *selects heavy books from the bookcase and lets them fall to the floor.*

She comes across a bible. She wipes the dust from it. She places her hand on it, looks at the floor, places it back on the bookcase.

She gathers the books on the floor into a pile. She stands on the pile, tests them with her weight.

She gets off the books.

She consults A5 speaking notes.

She goes to the sofa, sits briefly, gets up, walks slowly and graciously to the books, stands on them.

She looks out.

EVELYN. 'I am the mother of Michael Thomas.'

Clears her throat. Louder.

'I am the mother, of Michael Thomas.'

She looks at the clock.

She gets off the books, puts the cards down, leaves the room.

She enters with a birthday cake and two saucers. She puts them on the coffee table.

She puts the candles on the cake.

She pauses after the fifteenth candle.

Then continues.

(*Shouting out of the room.*) It's quarter to. I'm doing the cake now, Jas.

Silence.

You coming down?

A thumping noise is heard from upstairs.

EVELYN *waits for the thumping to finish.*

EVELYN *begins to light the many candles on the cake.*

The doorbell rings.

EVELYN *continues lighting the candles.*

The ringing becomes insistent.

The thumping starts up again.

EVELYN *goes to the window. Looks out. Comes back into the room.*

EVELYN *goes back to the window and looks out.*

The ringing of the bell is continuous and shrill.

She puts the chain on the front door.

She opens the front door partially. The thumping stops.

On the door step is JACKIE.

JACKIE.…I thought you was out, love. I was ringing and you weren't answering.

Beat.

I wouldn't have been ringing so hard if I'd of thought you was in…

Beat.

…I'd like to talk.

Silence.

Shall I come in then?

EVELYN *shuts the door.*

She goes into the front room and stares at the candlelit cake.

A long beat.

She blows the candles out.

She picks up an ornament from the bookcase. Holds it at her side.

She goes back to the front door. She releases the chain.

JACKIE *enters.*

She looks around, pensive.

The two women stare at one another.

Well, this is a lovely home, isn't it?

(*Looking around.*)…and… is there anyone else at home, with you?

EVELYN. Why wouldn't it be?

JACKIE. Sorry?

EVELYN. You sound surprised. Why wouldn't my home be 'lovely'?

JACKIE. No. I was just saying, love.

EVELYN. What were you saying?

JACKIE. I don't know.

(*Looking around.*) I suppose it's all very neutral and…

JACKIE *sees the cake.*

Oh. God. Sorry, love. You was celebrating. I didn't think you'd be celebrating, not today.

EVELYN. I wasn't celebrating.

JACKIE.… but you've got a cake, with candles?

EVELYN. I wasn't celebrating.

JACKIE. I could always come back another time. When it's a better time.

EVELYN. When would be a better time?

JACKIE. I couldn't rightly say. I guess... I wouldn't want to put you out... So, I probably wouldn't be coming back?

EVELYN. Well, you'd better stay, then, hadn't you?

JACKIE *sees the ornament in* EVELYN*'s hand.*

JACKIE *raises her own hands.*

JACKIE. I'm not looking for no trouble, love.

Beat.

EVELYN *puts the ornament down slowly on the table.*

JACKIE *turns away, looks to the window.*

Well, it's lovely outside, isn't it? So lovely when you get a bit of sunshine after all that rain. You'd never think you could have a day like today after such an awful morning, but here it is.

EVELYN. Yes?

JACKIE. Well, you remember me, don't you, love?

EVELYN. Why would I remember you?

EVELYN *looks straight at* JACKIE.

JACKIE. It was... you know?

EVELYN. No. I don't know.

JACKIE. Come on, love. You must know.

EVELYN. What must I know?

JACKIE *moves her hair from her face.*

JACKIE. D'you remember me now?

Beat.

Really...?

Pause.

Well, I suppose I have changed. Got older. Put on a bit of weight as you do and these lines. Bags. Hair thinner. You still look the same though. You don't look like you've changed.

EVELYN. Don't I?

Beat.

JACKIE. It's a compliment. Anyway, it was years ago. We were both…

EVELYN. We? You and I?

JACKIE. We were both…

EVELYN. Together?

JACKIE. Well it wasn't exactly 'together'. It was. We were…

EVELYN. We were?

JACKIE. No. 'We weren't'. It was you and it was me? But –

EVELYN. It was us, then?

JACKIE. No. No it wasn't 'us'.

EVELYN. Who was it then?

JACKIE. It was years ago…

Beat.

JACKIE *takes a deep breath.*

…I'm –

EVELYN. I remember you.

JACKIE *nodding, a nervous smile.*

There's something about that voice and that face has something about it too, but like you say you've probably aged. Quite a lot in fact, because I can't quite place you. But there is something. I just can't put my finger on it.

JACKIE *leaning in.*

I've got it. It's the eyes. They remind me of someone else's eyes. Whose eyes could they be, I wonder?

JACKIE....

EVELYN. But the thing is, I can't know you very well, if at all, because anyone who knows me at all would know not to come knocking on my door. Today of all days. But of course, you can't know what today is, can you?

Beat.

I thought I had you placed but no I don't think you can be the person I thought you were because if you were that person you wouldn't dare knock on my door today or any other day.

Beat.

So, you were going to tell me. Who are you again? You were about to say. 'You... are...'

EVELYN *leaning in*.

JACKIE....

EVELYN. Oh my goodness. I've got it now. You used to knock on the doors.

JACKIE. Do what?

EVELYN. You're a Witness.

JACKIE. I suppose... You could call it that.

EVELYN. A Jehovah's Witness...

JACKIE. Oh. No.

EVELYN. I remember you now.

JACKIE. No, I don't think you do.

EVELYN. My sister, Donna's a Witness. Perhaps you're from the same congregation.

JACKIE. No, I'm not.

EVELYN. Well, unlike some, I welcome you.

JACKIE.... You do?

EVELYN. Particularly as I've got some good news.

JACKIE.... Have you?

EVELYN. And you haven't come to do me any harm.

Beat.

But, oh I'm sorry, I've been rude. Would you like something to drink?

JACKIE. Oh. No.

EVELYN. Please.

JACKIE. A glass of water?

EVELYN. How about something stronger?

JACKIE. Oh, no I couldn't.

Beat.

I mean I would normally say, yes, but, I'm driving.

EVELYN (*nodding*). So you're a drinker, then?

Beat.

How about tea?

JACKIE. Tea?

EVELYN. How d'you like it?

JACKIE.... White. Two sugars, thanks.

EVELYN leaves the room.

The sound of a tap – water filling the kettle.

JACKIE uncertain.

A decision. JACKIE quickly adjusts herself trying to disappear a little bit.

JACKIE suddenly aware of the painting of MICHAEL.

Mesmerised.

The sound of the tap stopping.

EVELYN *re-enters.*

EVELYN. Why don't you take a seat.

JACKIE. Right.

JACKIE *takes a seat.* EVELYN *watching.*

Beat.

EVELYN. So?

JACKIE. You said you had some news?

EVELYN. I won't bother you with that.

JACKIE. It's no bother.

EVELYN. In that case, there's been a new development.

EVELYN *watching* JACKIE *closely.*

JACKIE. With what?

EVELYN. I can't talk about it until it's been properly announced. But let's just say… it's a 'compelling' development.

JACKIE. Compelling… In what way?

EVELYN. I've already said too much. Tell me about your God.

JACKIE. My God?

Beat.

Oh, well, he loves everyone, doesn't he?

EVELYN. Does he? Even people who do bad things? The worst of things?

JACKIE. I think so.

EVELYN. Can we talk about honesty? What have you got to say about that?

JACKIE. It's important? But… about that new development –

EVELYN. Are you an honest person?

JACKIE. Yes.

EVELYN. You always tell the truth, do you?

JACKIE. Yeah… most of the time. I'd like to know more about the development though –

EVELYN. Most of the time?

JACKIE. Well, we all tell little white lies every now and again, don't we?

EVELYN. Do we?

The sound of the kettle boiling.

Excuse me.

EVELYN *leaves.* JACKIE *watches her go.*

JACKIE *looks around the room.*

EVELYN *re-enters with a cup of tea.*

JACKIE. Oh, thank you, ta, love.

JACKIE *takes the tea. Sips.*

EVELYN *watches.*

EVELYN. Let's continue shall we? So?

JACKIE. You said an 'important development'. What is it?

EVELYN. Like I said, I can't say much about it now.

JACKIE *shifts.*

But I can say for certain what's going to happen as a consequence of it.

JACKIE. For certain? Well, go on then.

EVELYN. It's going to flush out all those cowards who currently fester in their rotting holes.

Beat.

Those gutless cowards who stay unaccountable for their evil deeds. They, and their families, are going to be so blinded by the light, when they are finally brought to the light (and they will be brought to the light), that they would rather wish they were dead.

Judgment is going to rain down upon them without any mercy. Let's just say this new development is going to change... everything.

Beat.

JACKIE. All that. Blimey!

But... people 'often' say that, don't they? That 'Something's gonna change something else'. But when you get down to the nuts and bolts of it, it's all just the same, really – nothing's changed. And the people that keep saying it, well, you've got to question their sanity really haven't you, if they keep saying it, which they do, like a broken record.

Maybe, something's not right with them... Maybe they've got a problem.

Beat.

I feel quite sorry for them, really. Except that what they're doing is wasting everybody's time proving what we already know to be the case – that there is nothing new.

EVELYN. Well, we'll just have to wait and see, won't we.

Beat.

Have you got children?

JACKIE. Yeah, I've got a son.

EVELYN. You have.

Beat.

And what does your son do now?

JACKIE. He fixes cars. Anything that's broken he can fix it. He's very good at fixing things.

EVELYN. Doing well for himself, then?

JACKIE. Does very well for himself. Keeps to himself. Gets on very well with his boss and his work mates. Doesn't have no trouble. Has all sorts of friends. Lives a good life. Lives a quiet life. Just an ordinary lad really.

EVELYN. Ordinary? And he lives with you?

JACKIE. Oh no. Just moved in with his girlfriend. Gemma. Nice enough girl. Speaking of which…

JACKIE pauses then goes to her bag.

Takes out her mobile and pulls up a picture. Shows EVELYN.

If EVELYN *is standing she'll need to sit.*

That's Gemma. Had their ups and downs but they're settled now. Into their own place. What they can afford. A young couple just starting out. As a mum you wish them all the very best don't you?

EVELYN. She's pregnant.

JACKIE. Their first…

JACKIE slides to a scan picture.

…She's at the stage where anything can go wrong. You just don't want them to have any stresses, do you? No added pressures on their backs. Because stress can come from all sorts of places, can't it? It can come from digging up the past and from the things people say about the past – which, is all in the past now anyway. There's nothing 'new' about the past, is there? So there's no changing it. No point raising it. No point destroying lives… 'cause of it.

Beat.

As mums we both know how important life is, don't we?

EVELYN. Fragile.

JACKIE. But this here is new life and new life hasn't got to pay for our mistakes.

EVELYN. Mistakes?

JACKIE. None of us is perfect.

Beat.

…And, no one wants to cause a miscarriage, do they?

Beat.

Imagine being that person. Who could live with that? Having an innocent baby's blood on your hands… So… Thanks for letting me in.

JACKIE *gets her bag. Tea cup in hand.*

God bless and all that…

EVELYN (*sniggers*). You've barely been here five minutes. Do you even know my name? I didn't get yours.

JACKIE.… We weren't doing that. Names are not important, are they?

EVELYN. It's Evelyn.

JACKIE *stops.*

Evelyn Thomas. And my son. He's in the picture.

EVELYN *directs* JACKIE *to the picture on the wall.*

Michael. Michael Thomas.

EVELYN *studies* JACKIE *for a reaction. It's slow to come.*

Recognise him?

JACKIE. As I say it's not important to know.

EVELYN. Look at him. Look. At. Him. Michael Thomas. Michael… Thomas. He was coming from the library.

JACKIE *doesn't look.*

JACKIE. Was he?

EVELYN. He was attacked.

JACKIE.… Sorry to hear that.

EVELYN. And killed.

JACKIE.... Oh.

EVELYN. Do you remember him now?

JACKIE. If I'd of known it was gonna distress you, love...

EVELYN. You wouldn't have come knocking on my door, to tell me your good news?

Beat.

It's not catching... murder.

JACKIE. I'm sorry.

EVELYN. What have you got to be sorry about?

JACKIE. I should be going... I've disturbed you enough already.

EVELYN. No. I think you should stay.

JACKIE *nearing the door.*

Don't you want to hear about the new development?

JACKIE *stops.*

Have another cup of tea, then. Let me fill you up. White. Two sugars.

EVELYN *takes* JACKIE*'s cup, brushes past* JACKIE *and leaves the room.*

JACKIE *sits down reluctantly.*

Michael's picture looms.

JACKIE *squirms to resist looking at it.*

JACKIE*'s mobile bleeps a message.*

JACKIE *studies the message.*

She types in two words.

The whoosh of the send button.

EVELYN *returns with another cup of tea.*

So tea...

EVELYN *gives the cup to* JACKIE.

JACKIE *takes a sip*.

Good?

JACKIE *nods*.

I left the bag in.

JACKIE. I can see.

JACKIE *takes a further sip*.

EVELYN *watches*.

EVELYN *licks her lips*.

EVELYN. I think you can really help me.

JACKIE. I don't think I can.

EVELYN. I've got to give a speech.

JACKIE. You've 'got' to give a speech?

EVELYN. To mark the anniversary of Michael's death – it's fifteen years. And there are some things I'm just not sure about. You could help me with those things.

JACKIE. I'm not much good with speeches. Never had to give any and I don't think there's anything I can help you with.

EVELYN. It won't be long.

EVELYN *adjusts the pile of books in the middle of the room. She clears her throat.*

So, it starts with the getting up and going bit.

JACKIE. The getting up and going bit?

EVELYN *sits down, gets up, walks to the books and stands on them.*

She practices again. This time slower. More dignified, head raised.

Don't you just get up and go?

EVELYN (*sniggers*). That would be a mistake. Everyone's

watching me. Looking at how I'm walking and what I'm wearing – what my face looks like: 'Has she got on any make up?' 'Has she got on too much?', 'What's she done with her hair?' All those tiny judgements could trip me up.

JACKIE. I see.

EVELYN. But do you? Because that's not the worst part.

JACKIE. What's the worst part?

EVELYN. CP I call it.

JACKIE. CP?

EVELYN. Collective pity. You gave me yours. Imagine this, I'm in a room with a hundred people and they're all giving me their pity. Can you imagine the weight of all of that pity? It's so heavy and it's really really really sad and I've got to take that enormous hunk of a thing with me and carry it as I go up to the place where I've got to give my speech.

JACKIE. You don't want anyone's pity?

EVELYN. That's not the point. They're going to give it to me whether I want it or not. The point is balance.

JACKIE. I see.

EVELYN. But, do you?

Beat.

Because, it doesn't just matter for me. I'm not the only one going up there to give my speech.

JACKIE. Who else is going with you?

EVELYN. Michael.

JACKIE. Your dead son?

EVELYN *nods*.

Oh… right – I think I had better be going.

JACKIE *starts to gather her things*.

EVELYN. He can't physically represent himself can he? If I go and mess it up I'm messing it up for him. The way I am and the way people see me walking up to that place is how they'll see him. 'Oh there's that dead boy's mum who tripped up on the way to give her speech. No wonder what happened happened – if the mum can't even walk properly…'

Do you see where I'm coming from?

Thumping is heard from the ceiling upstairs. JACKIE looks up at the ceiling.

Give it a minute.

JACKIE. What's that?

EVELYN. Nothing.

JACKIE. Don't sound like nothing.

EVELYN. My son.

JACKIE.…I really should be going.

EVELYN. My eldest. The one that's not dead.

JACKIE. He's here?

EVELYN. That's right.

JACKIE. Upstairs? But you said.

EVELYN. I never said.

JACKIE. What's he doing upstairs?

EVELYN. Wants something.

JACKIE. And that's how he tells you?

EVELYN. Bangs on the floor.

JACKIE. Why does he do that?

EVELYN. Give it a minute.

They both wait for the thumping to stop. It stops.

JACKIE. Well, I really should be going.

EVELYN. Do we make you feel uncomfortable?

JACKIE *looks to the door.*

I'll continue, then.

JACKIE *continues looking at the door.*

Let's do the beginning.

JACKIE*'s mobile bleeps.* JACKIE *looks at it.*

EVELYN *stands on the podium.*

(*To* JACKIE.) Are you listening?

JACKIE *puts the mobile away.*

'I'm deeply humbled by your presence. Thank you for coming.'

The thumping noise starts again.

Excuse me.

EVELYN *goes to the cake. She cuts a slice, puts it on a saucer and leaves the room with it.*

The sound of her feet going up stairs.

JACKIE *gets out her mobile, speed dials.*

JACKIE.... You're at Granddad's...?

You're with Mark...?

No, love, I wouldn't embarrass you...

Yeah, course. I'm just sorting a few things out. I'll get there as soon as I can.

EVELYN *re-enters the room. Watches* JACKIE.

JACKIE*'s tone is changed:*

Alright, then... yep... Got to go. Love to Gem. See you in a tick.

JACKIE *listens. Clicks off her phone.*

EVELYN. Everything alright?

JACKIE. Yeah, you?

EVELYN *nods. She gets back into position.*

EVELYN. So, where was I?

JACKIE. You was saying thank you.

EVELYN. 'Thank you all for coming.'

JACKIE. Who's coming?

EVELYN. It's friends, family, well-wishers, more 'do-gooders', some press.

JACKIE. What press?

EVELYN. The local gazette and national.

JACKIE. National?

EVELYN. It's been fifteen years, and what with the new 'development' there's bound to be interest.

JACKIE. About that?

EVELYN. I haven't finished. And next I mention Michael.

JACKIE. What you gonna say about him?

EVELYN. 'Of course I can't give a speech like this without thanking my beautiful son. I can hear him in my ear now. He's saying "Mum, you're embarrassing me."'

JACKIE. That's what they say, don't they?

JACKIE*'s mobile bleeps a message.* JACKIE *looks at her mobile.*

EVELYN. 'When people ask me "what was he like?", I say bright, inquisitive, studious. He had this way about him, a knowingness. He could look right into your soul. I truly believe he was sent from God, I truly believe that he's an angel. He was perfect...'

JACKIE *turns her back to the picture and scratches her neck.*

Next, I think I should ask the audience a question. Something like:

'Can I have a show of hands for anyone that's lost someone dear to them.'

JACKIE. We've all lost someone dear to us, haven't we?

EVELYN. Yes, but it's making a connection and saying 'it's not just me' and once I've made that connection, I'll say: 'Losing a loved one is terribly hard.'

JACKIE. I lost my dad.

EVELYN. You did.

JACKIE. But he was eighty-seven. A good age as they say.

EVELYN. And then I'll say, 'Losing a child is worse than any loss you can ever imagine.'

JACKIE*'s mobile bleeps a message.* JACKIE *looks at her mobile.*

JACKIE *considers.*

'Most of you know what happened to me.'

JACKIE *is distracted.*

So. What d'you think of it so far?

JACKIE *back in the room.*

JACKIE. What? I don't know.

EVELYN. Well, is there anything you'd change? What about the tone?

JACKIE. It's your speech, love.

EVELYN. But I'm asking you.

JACKIE. Like I said speeches aren't my thing. No one's never asked me to give any.

EVELYN. And why is that?

JACKIE. Maybe people don't want to hear what I've got to say.

EVELYN. Well this is your chance then, isn't it? What would you change if it were you giving it?

JACKIE. I wouldn't be giving it.

EVELYN. But let's pretend.

Beat.

JACKIE. Well, it's a bit...

EVELYN. Yes?

JACKIE. ...Depressing.

EVELYN. Depressing?

JACKIE. And I'm not sure...

EVELYN. Yes?

JACKIE. If people really want to hear that now? It has been fifteen years.

EVELYN. So you're saying, you wouldn't give the speech?

JACKIE. I'm saying you don't have to give the speech.

EVELYN. Yes I do.

JACKIE. No you don't.

EVELYN. Yes, I do.

JACKIE. Not from where I'm sitting, you don't.

Beat.

You seem to care so much about what people think. All the 'getting up and going' malarkey. What if people are just being polite?

EVELYN. If you were me, you'd let people forget?

JACKIE. Forgetting might'n be such a bad thing... I mean for everyone, to just sort of move on... including you.

EVELYN. Move on?

EVELYN *gets off the podium and goes to the shelves. She pulls out loose pictures from a box/album and spreads them over part of the coffee table.*

EVELYN *picks up a picture.*

JACKIE *over her shoulder.*

…

EVELYN *picks up another picture.*

…

Picks up another picture.

First day of school.

Picks up another picture.

His tenth birthday.

Picks up another picture.

Florida.

(*Directly to* JACKIE.) How do I move on?

JACKIE. I didn't mean…

EVELYN *gathers the pictures and puts them back in the box/album and on the shelf.*

Why don't you make it more about the good things then, a… celebration.

EVELYN. A celebration?

JACKIE. Of his life.

EVELYN. How would I do that?

JACKIE. Well, to start off with you probably wouldn't want to say much about… you know… the…

EVELYN. Murder?

JACKIE. And I'd start with something more… uplifting.

EVELYN. What would you do to make a speech about my
    murdered son more 'uplifting'?

JACKIE. Well, it's just an idea.

EVELYN. What's the idea?

JACKIE. You might not like it.

    Beat.

    You could tell a joke?

EVELYN. A joke?

JACKIE. No listen, my dad did loads of speeches 'cause he did
    the raffles at the Legion, and he always started with a joke
    and it was the same joke every time.

EVELYN. What was the joke?

JACKIE. Um... No. I can't remember it.

EVELYN. But it was always the same. What was it?

JACKIE.... It wouldn't be funny now.

EVELYN. But you laughed then?

JACKIE. Why don't you try and come up with a joke for your
    speech. Maybe about someone who's going to be there when
    you're giving it. Your family that you mentioned? What
    family is going to be there?

EVELYN. My sister. Donna.

JACKIE. What's funny about her?

    EVELYN *thinks*.

EVELYN. She still cries, and when she cries it's this big wailing
    noise. It sounds like a foghorn.

    EVELYN *illustrates*.

    Time doesn't seem to have weathered her wailing.

JACKIE.... Anybody else?

EVELYN. My ex-husband.

JACKIE. Ex-husbands are always good for a laugh.

EVELYN. Not my ex-husband.

JACKIE. Why not?

EVELYN. Because it would become about 'us' and why we don't talk any more.

JACKIE. What about something funny that's happened to you recently, then?

EVELYN. Something funny did happen to me recently.

JACKIE. Go on.

EVELYN. I was in the supermarket and an old woman stopped me.

JACKIE. What did she look like?

EVELYN. Little with beady eyes.

JACKIE. Say that then. That sounds a bit funny 'Little with beady eyes'.

EVELYN. 'So I was in the supermarket and a little old woman with little beady eyes stopped me.'

JACKIE. What was she wearing?

EVELYN. I can't remember now, maybe a trench coat.

JACKIE. Say that then, too.

EVELYN. 'So I was in the supermarket and a little old woman with little beady eyes and a trench coat stopped me. And she said, "Don't I know you from somewhere? You look familiar."'

JACKIE. Go on.

EVELYN. '"Oh I know," she said. She was looking at me directly and she said, "I saw you on the telly."'

Silence.

JACKIE. Well? And?

EVELYN. And that's it.

JACKIE. What's funny about that?

EVELYN. I have been on the TV.

JACKIE. And? What's funny then?

EVELYN. Shall I give you a clue?

>EVELYN *stands on the makeshift podium. Takes a deep breath. Clenches her fists.*

>'If anyone knows anything, anything, then please come forward. Please give that information to the police. I'm begging you.'

JACKIE.… Oh.

EVELYN. So thanks for your suggestion but I can't do jokes.

JACKIE. I can see that.

EVELYN. It's awkward. There'd be a pause. No one would laugh.

JACKIE. I can see that.

EVELYN. So I'll just continue, then.
>'Most of you know what happened to me. On 10th November 2005, my son, Michael, who had just turned fifteen, left our house. He was just going up the road to meet his friend. They were going to the library.'

>JACKIE *looks in her bag, fiddling with something.*

>What?

JACKIE. Nothing.

>JACKIE *waves* EVELYN *to continue.*

>You go on.

>JACKIE *continues to fiddle in her bag.*

EVELYN. What is it?

JACKIE. Maybe, I just think, you shouldn't say the 'going to the library' bit.

EVELYN. But he was going to the library.

JACKIE. That's what he 'told' you that he was doing.

EVELYN. That is what he told me and that is what he did.

JACKIE. But maybe he was going somewhere else. You wouldn't know, would you? He could have been up to all sorts.

EVELYN. All sorts like what?

JACKIE. I don't know.

EVELYN. What do you think my son was doing?

JACKIE. It doesn't matter.

EVELYN. Yes, it does.

JACKIE. It's just some people might think...

EVELYN. Think what?

JACKIE. A boy like that –

EVELYN. A boy like what?

JACKIE. Well... even if you just based it on all the stuff in the news. What all the facts and figures show. It's good to be... realistic. Thinking about... what was the most likeliest thing that your son might have been doing.

EVELYN. What are you talking about?

JACKIE. So, well maybe, he might... for instance, have been out... in the park... mugging people...

A sharp inhalation of breath from EVELYN.

Well, you just don't know, do you?

A deep silence from EVELYN.

A long beat as EVELYN *shakes her head in disbelief.*

EVELYN *gets off the makeshift podium.*

Looks at the ornament she left on the table, she touches it.

EVELYN. You think the murder of my son was justified.

JACKIE (*defensive*). I never said that.

EVELYN. Do you think he deserved to die?

JACKIE. I didn't say that.

EVELYN *comes up close to* JACKIE

My son went to the library. Do you understand me?

EVELYN *composes herself and goes slowly back onto the podium.*

EVELYN. And I'll continue.

Looks at her cards. Grabs on hard to them.

'At 8:30 p.m. I called his best friend's mum. Michael wasn't with his best friend. He wasn't with any friends. He wasn't with his brother. He wasn't at his dad's. My mum hadn't seen him all day either.'

JACKIE.... You're talking about the playground.

EVELYN. What playground?

JACKIE. When they're little. You're in the playground and they're on the swings. You look away, just for one minute, and the next thing you know they've gone and your shitting it. That's what you're talking about.

Beat.

What are you going to say next?

EVELYN. I'm going to say why I think he was killed.

JACKIE. But you haven't said he was killed yet. You're saving that bit?

EVELYN. Saving it for what?

JACKIE. The end.

EVELYN. I'm not 'saving it'. It's why we're all still here.

EVELYN *clears her throat again.*

'I believe the attack on my son was motivated by racism.'

The thumping starts up again.

EVELYN *looks at the clock.*

JACKIE. Hold on.

EVELYN. 'There can be no other explanation.'

JACKIE. Because he was black?

EVELYN. I believe his killers were racists.

The thumping continues getting louder.

JACKIE. But you don't know that. You weren't there.

EVELYN. 'I believe their families are racists.'

JACKIE. No. You can't say that.

EVELYN. 'I believe the police who were investigating, were racists.'

JACKIE. Oh, please. It could just have been self-defence.

EVELYN. It was racism.

JACKIE. He could just have been in the wrong place at the wrong time.

EVELYN. It was racism.

The thumping becomes intense.

JACKIE *gathers her bag to go.*

I haven't finished.

JACKIE. Got somewhere to be.

EVELYN (*shouting up at the ceiling*). Jason, stop!

The thumping gets lighter then stops.

(*To* JACKIE.) You need to hear the rest.

JACKIE *going to the door.*

EVELYN *gets off the podium.*

EVELYN *touches* JACKIE'*s arm.*

JACKIE. Don't touch me.

Beat.

Why is it so easy for you to say that word?

EVELYN. What word?

JACKIE. The 'R' word.

EVELYN. 'Racist'?

JACKIE (*flinches*). You lot throw that word around like it's going out of fashion.

EVELYN. What's wrong with using the word 'racist'?

JACKIE. When you say that word it stops us from talking. It's not a fair word. It only means one thing.

EVELYN. Are you a racist?

JACKIE. No.

EVELYN. But your father was with his jokes?

JACKIE. No he wasn't.

EVELYN. You sure?

JACKIE. His jokes was harmless.

EVELYN. They were seeds.

JACKIE. If an old man believes in this country does that make him a 'racist'?

EVELYN. Your father and your son close were they?

JACKIE. Yes. If you must know. And?

EVELYN. Seeds grow… take root… and become…

EVELYN *gets back on the podium.*

'Killers – The killers of my son preyed on an innocent
talented young boy. The killers of my son are evil, barbaric
cowards. And I curse them.'

JACKIE. Hold on.

EVELYN. I curse their families, and in particular the mothers
that raised them.

JACKIE. You can't do that.

EVELYN. I can, and I do.

JACKIE. What if it isn't black and white?

EVELYN. Michael's dead.

JACKIE. But you should look deeper.

EVELYN. There's nothing else to see.

JACKIE. Because you're not looking. Say they were really just
defending themselves – those 'evil' killers.

EVELYN. No one needed to 'defend' themselves against my
son.

JACKIE. Michael was a big lad for his age? Towered above you
I bet? Had a temper?

EVELYN. You wouldn't find a more gentle soul.

JACKIE. Say it was just a split-second thing. It wasn't meant to
happen.

EVELYN. Like an accident?

JACKIE. Could have been.

EVELYN. How do you stab a person fifteen times, with a
six-inch knife by accident?

JACKIE. Was the knife six inches?

EVELYN. Yes it was.

Beat.

JACKIE. Say, then, the killers was gullible, easily led –

EVELYN. Do any of them have medical conditions?

JACKIE. No.

EVELYN. Evil.

JACKIE. Say the killers of Michael was kids themselves?

EVELYN. How old?

JACKIE. Seventeen, maybe eighteen.

EVELYN. Then they were adults and evil.

JACKIE. Say they was pushed to the limit.

EVELYN. By what?

JACKIE. By what was around them.

EVELYN. Irrelevant. Say they were damaged. Say they were
bullied at twelve and expelled at thirteen. Say they got
in with the wrong crowd. Say their mothers were totally
incompetent and never raised them properly. Say on the
morning of the murder they got out of the wrong side of the
bed. Say it was a Monday and they didn't like Mondays.
Irrelevant. They killed my son. And I curse them.

Beat.

The thumping on the ceiling starts up again.

I curse their future generations.

JACKIE. No, you don't.

EVELYN. Yes I do. I curse their babies in the womb.

JACKIE. No, you don't.

EVELYN. Yes I do. I pray that they mutate, become severely
deformed and never breathe one breath of air. I pray they are
born dead.

Beat.

Yes, I pray that they are miscarried.

The thumping gets louder and picks up pace.

JACKIE. You don't mean that. There's a problem and the problem is with people like you. You don't get it.

EVELYN. I don't get what?

JACKIE. If I was going to give your speech this is what I'd say… I'd say

'Learn the lessons.'

EVELYN. What lessons?

JACKIE. For them young lads –

The thumping becomes relentless and intense.

EVELYN. What young lads?

JACKIE. Just any young lads. Life might not have been going their way. Bottom of the pile; buses full of your people speaking their gobbledygook; won't show their bloody hair (who wants to see it? Not us!); no jobs, NHS blocked up with your people and their smell, taking the piss; you send your kids to school (if you can get them into one that is) and no one speaks bloody English and we've all got to celebrate Ramadan –

EVELYN. What you're saying makes no sense. We have a right to be here. My 'people', whoever you think that might be, built, and continue to build, 'our' country. Who is it that drives your buses? Who are your doctors? Who are your nurses and teachers? There's no logic to what you are saying.

JACKIE. I'm just saying the truth.

EVELYN. Well, then your 'truth' is flawed and you are a racist.

JACKIE. You can't say that.

The thumping is frenzied.

EVELYN. Can't I…? I'll put it another way then: you are an ignorant, bigoted, white woman.

JACKIE. How dare you? D'you know what? You're the racist.

EVELYN *laughs and her laughs turns into something else.*

JACKIE *looks at* EVELYN *as if she's mad.*

I was saying that what happened to your Michael might just have been something that bubbled over after years building up. It might have been just a second.It might have been about survival and defending themselves from being wiped out and being at the bottom of the bloody pile and watching it all slip away.

And you've got to look at what come before and what comes after. What was in the middle might just have been a mistake.

EVELYN. A mistake?

JACKIE. A mistake that was bound to happen. But, a mistake all the same.

EVELYN. 'There's black and white, evil and innocence, life and death. There is no half way house. You cannot excuse the actions of a murderer by his circumstances… or his ignorance. Those that killed my son are pure evil and will always be. You can't divorce the act from the person.'

Beat.

And people like you are full of excuses for them. It's always somebody else's fault.

EVELYN *leaves the room. She goes to the foot of the stairs.*

(*Shouting upstairs.*) Jas, stop. I'll be up in a minute.

There are a few defiant thumps and then they stop.

EVELYN *comes back into the room.*

JACKIE*'s phone rings. She answers it.*

JACKIE.…I'm coming, love… I'm leaving right now… I'm getting in the car. Call me in a couple of minutes.

JACKIE *ends the call.*

EVELYN. You've got to go.

JACKIE. I've got to go.

JACKIE *gathers her belongings.*

EVELYN. But before you do, you'll want to hear the end of the speech. I've added a new bit.

EVELYN *steps back on the makeshift podium. Prepares.*

'Fourteen years ago four men, four murderers, were put on trial for killing my son. Their names –

JACKIE. They were boys. You can't say their names like that. That's not right.

EVELYN. They were men. And this time I will say their names.

Beat.

'The murderers' names –

JACKIE. That's blasphemy.

EVELYN. Are they gods to you?

Beat.

Don't you mean defamatory?

JACKIE. Yeah, that.

EVELYN. Well guess what, I don't care any more. 'The murderers' names are:

Beat.

Mark Colson, Jimmy Gibbs, Lewis Gibbs… and Daniel Miller.'

JACKIE. They were found not guilty.

EVELYN. They got away with murder.

JACKIE. They was innocent.

EVELYN. Was?

JACKIE. Are.

JACKIE *distracted by* MICHAEL*'s picture.*

EVELYN. All I want is justice for Michael. All I want is the truth, Jackie.

JACKIE *looks at* EVELYN.

Did you think I'd make it easy for you? I sat in the same court room. Watched as you gave your son reassurance, nodded to him, blew him kisses. Of course I know your bloody face.

Beat.

I watched as you and your father punched the air when the verdict was read.

Silence

Why did you knock on my door? To rub salt?

JACKIE. No. Of course not.

EVELYN. To break bread?

JACKIE. No.

EVELYN. To make friends, then?

JACKIE. No.

EVELYN. Did you want me to put you in the speech?

JACKIE. No.

EVELYN (*lowering her tone*). 'One of the mothers of the men who was acquitted of my son's murder came to visit me on the fifteenth anniversary of his death, on his birthday.'

JACKIE. Stop it.

EVELYN. 'She sat in my front room and on my sofa.'

JACKIE. I don't want to be in your speech.

EVELYN. What did you come for, then? Did you want some cake?

EVELYN *puts a slice of the cake on a saucer and holds it out to* JACKIE.

Have some of Michael's cake, Jackie.

JACKIE *staring at it.*

I dare you.

JACKIE. I thought you and me could talk. Because, at the end of the day, we're both mums.

EVELYN *sniggers*.

Hold on. Let me show you something.

JACKIE *rushes to her bag, rifling through it. She takes out a picture*.

I went through my dad's stuff, clearing it out. He's got so much stuff.

Beat.

I found this in one of his albums.

EVELYN *glances at it quickly and looks away*.

There's Dan.

Nodding smiling, wiping the picture.

He'd just had his birthday that April and we went away in the June. Look at his hair.

EVELYN. I don't want to look at his hair.

JACKIE. Used to call him Goldilocks 'cause of that hair. Soft, you could barely feel it in your hands.

Beat.

That holiday we couldn't get him out the bloody water. Look at his face. What d'you see in that face?

Trying to put the picture in front of EVELYN. EVELYN *turns away*.

That's innocence. That's my little boy on the best holiday of his life.

JACKIE *goes back to her bag and pulls out an old small blanket*.

This was his. Dad had it.

JACKIE *smells it.*

He slept with it every night till he was eleven. This is where he used to chew it. See?

Kids. They put everything in their mouths don't they?

I never knew where this old thing went. Dad must have slipped it away when we weren't looking.

(*Puts on a husky cockney voice.*) 'A man don't need blankets. You ain't a mummy's boy no more.'

JACKIE *goes back into her bag takes out a small football trophy.*

EVELYN *puts the saucer down.*

EVELYN. If this is what you've come for, Jackie. I don't need it.

JACKIE. Dad's got loads and loads of these all round the house. Medals and trophies that I can't even remember. Dad kept all Dan's trophies.

Beat.

He was proud of his boy…

JACKIE *freezes.*

EVELYN. What?

JACKIE *quickly puts the trophy back in her bag.*

JACKIE. You and me we're the same. We're just mums. So you can understand, can't you? Please just leave us be now, Evelyn. Let us live our lives.

JACKIE *gathers her things to go.*

EVELYN. They found new DNA.

JACKIE. What?

EVELYN. And it's going to change everything.

JACKIE *shaking her head.*

JACKIE. There was already DNA. They was all in the park, remember? There's nothing new in that.

EVELYN. Not their DNA… someone else's.

JACKIE. Whose?

EVELYN. A new witness. Someone who must have been there and seen what they did.

JACKIE. You're lying.

EVELYN. Why would I lie?

JACKIE. Whose is it, then?

EVELYN.…

JACKIE. Like I said nothing new.

EVELYN. A woman.

JACKIE. A woman?

EVELYN. Yes, there was a woman present. And now there'll have to be a whole new investigation, Jackie. It's going to be all over the news again and she'll come forward and confirm what your son and those other animals did to my son.

Beat.

JACKIE. And you honestly believe that? That this 'woman' if she exists, after fifteen years is gonna suddenly appear from nowhere and pipe up and say. 'Oh, yeah I forgot after all this time, I was there'?

Beat.

You're living in cloud cuckoo land, love… How d'you know it wasn't her, this woman that killed your son? In fact, this is good news for us, isn't it? This is great news because it proves my son is innocent.

EVELYN. I dream about you. You and those rats being back in that court room and being back on that stand and having your lies destroyed. I can't wait for that day and it's coming.

JACKIE. Oh bollocks! We can't breathe. With your digging and bloody speeches and 'new developments'. Just when we start to think this is finally over, up you bloody pop again with something else. At least you get pity. Every time you pop up, we get hate.

Beat.

Whatever it is you keep searching for, isn't there. I'm sorry what happened happened to you but leave my Dan and them boys alone now, Evelyn. Isn't it time you just stopped raking it up?

EVELYN *starts to slow clap.*

EVELYN. Do you know what it's like to bury a child, Jackie?

Beat.

You watch as this box, this coffin, that you've picked out, containing your child, your flesh, your blood, is lowered into the ground. They shovel dirt on top of dirt on top of dirt. Shovelling, shovelling, shovelling, shovelling, shovelling, shovelling, this dirt on top of this wooden box that's been lowered into the ground that contains your child. Do you know what you're doing?

You're screaming. Nobody can hear you. They're shovelling and you're screaming.

You want to jump in that hole and open that box because you know and every bone in your body is telling you that your child cannot be in that box. He's not in that box. D'you know why he can't be in that box? Because he's just turned fifteen and he's still got a present to open.

Beat.

Because he's got his homework to do. Because his room's a tip and he needs to clean it properly.

Beat.

There is nothing that will stop me from 'raking it up'. And you and I are not the same. About 'we mums'. There is no 'we' in this. 'We' do not have any kind of connection on any kind of level. Now get out.

JACKIE. What more do you want, Evelyn?

EVELYN. Answers.

JACKIE. I can give you them. If that's what will get you off our backs, here I am, ask away.

EVELYN. You wouldn't answer my questions.

JACKIE. If it meant you'd stop. Once and for all, then I would.

EVELYN. You couldn't answer anything honestly.

JACKIE. Try me.

Beat.

EVELYN. Right then.

EVELYN begins re-arranging the furniture. Moving the sofa. Dragging the coffee table (making a court room).

JACKIE. What you doing?

EVELYN puts the pile of books in the middle of the room again.

EVELYN clears her throat.

EVELYN. Jackie Miller?

EVELYN directs JACKIE to get on the books.

JACKIE. Oh for heaven's sake.

EVELYN stares at the books.

JACKIE stands on the books.

EVELYN searches for and gets the bible from the bookcase.

She gives it to JACKIE to hold, which JACKIE does awkwardly.

EVELYN. Do you swear, by Almighty God, to tell the truth, the whole truth and nothing but the truth?

JACKIE shrugs.

Say it.

JACKIE. Yeah, whatever.

EVELYN. On the night of 10th November 2005, between 9 p.m. and midnight, where were you?

JACKIE *clears her throat.*

JACKIE. At home.

EVELYN. What were you doing?

JACKIE. It's hard to say. It was fourteen years ago. I can't remember the detail.

EVELYN. You made a statement. What did your statement say?

JACKIE. It said I was at home that I cooked dinner, did some ironing and watched TV.

EVELYN. Did you consume any alcohol?

JACKIE. That's not relevant. My statement never said nothing about that.

EVELYN. Exactly, it didn't. So did you have a drink?

JACKIE. It was fifteen years ago.

EVELYN. When you're at home doing the ironing and watching the TV, do you have a drink?

JACKIE. This isn't relevant.

EVELYN. I bet you do. When I offered you something stronger you said: 'I would normally say yes but I'm driving.'

JACKIE *scoffs.*

JACKIE. You was trying to trip me up?

EVELYN. So, we can say, based on your normal pattern of behaviour, that when you were at home fifteen years ago on the evening of the 10th November you would have had a drink. Maybe more than one drink and drink dulls the senses. You probably nodded off.

JACKIE. I didn't nod off!

EVELYN. And you're sure about that?

JACKIE. Definitely.

EVELYN. So you can't remember the 'details' of that night but you definitely know you didn't fall asleep.

JACKIE shifts.

JACKIE. Yeah.

Beat.

Is this what you've been waiting for, Evelyn? Longing for all these years? Because of course, you would have done it better than anyone else? Typical. How long did it take you to come up with that?

EVELYN. In your statement you said your son, Daniel Miller, was at home with you all evening into the night.

JACKIE. That's what it says.

EVELYN. All evening and into the night? In the same room?

JACKIE. Some of the time.

EVELYN. So if it was only some of the time how d'you know he was at home all evening and into the night?

JACKIE. After all these years, is that all you've got? How d'you know your son upstairs is upstairs?

Beat.

As I said, fifteen years ago and as I say now, Dan was at home with me, all evening.

EVELYN. Yes, but did you lie?

JACKIE. A whole court decided they was innocent, Evelyn… There is nothing else.

EVELYN *lost for words.*

Is that it, then?

Beat.

JACKIE *gets off the books*.

EVELYN. I'll tell everyone where you live.

JACKIE. You don't know that.

EVELYN. Flat 46, Winchester Court.

JACKIE. You [know where I live]?

EVELYN. And now I know he's moved, I'll find out his new address; 'Scum' written all over the front door; people spitting in his path as he's pushing the buggy? That will be nice, won't it?

JACKIE. We had an agreement.

EVELYN. You've given me nothing. I can tell everyone where he works as well.

Beat.

Prestige Autos, is it? Corner of the High Street? Employers don't like that kind of bad publicity do they? People driving past and calling out profanities from their car windows.

JACKIE. I have got something.

Beat.

The DNA person you lot are looking for, it wasn't a woman.

EVELYN *scoffs*.

EVELYN. You can't argue with the science, Jackie. It's already been proven. It was a woman.

JACKIE.... It was a girl.

Beat.

EVELYN. How would you know that?

JACKIE. No. I can't say no more.

EVELYN. Why would you say that if you can't say any more...? What d'you know?

JACKIE. She don't change nothing, Evelyn.

EVELYN. Tell me who she is then.

JACKIE. You're barking up the wrong tree, is all I'm saying. If she is who I think she is, she ain't coming forwards for no one.

EVELYN. What do you know, Jackie?

JACKIE *shaking her head.*

JACKIE. No… I've said too much already and I'll deny I ever said that.

EVELYN (*exasperated*). Please.

Beat.

I'm begging you.

Beat.

Who was this girl?

JACKIE *shakes her head.*

JACKIE. Do what you want. Tell everyone where we live. I'm not saying no more.

EVELYN. You know what this means to me.

EVELYN *gets down on her knees.*

EVELYN *reaches slowly out to* JACKIE*'s foot.*

Please…

JACKIE *looks at her.*

JACKIE. I can't. I'm sorry.

JACKIE *starts to leave.*

EVELYN. I have a confession. For fourteen long years I've cursed you, your family and those other boys and their families. They sat in the dock like butter wouldn't melt and you shielded them.

JACKIE. Because… my son was innocent.

EVELYN. I've been angry.

JACKIE. That's understandable I suppose. I would have been too. What you've been through all that heartache.

EVELYN. I spat in your tea. I gathered up the phlegm in my mouth with as much bile and anger and hatred as I could muster and I spat it into your tea and I used my unwashed finger and I swirled it in. And I watched you drink it, white, two sugars and my spit.

JACKIE. I need the bathroom.

EVELYN. Did it taste nice?

JACKIE. Please?

EVELYN. Down the hall, on the left.

JACKIE exits.

Retching and spitting can be heard offstage.

JACKIE's mobile starts ringing.

EVELYN locates it.

Answers it.

…No I'm not your mum…

…My name is Evelyn. Evelyn Thomas. And I know what you did.

The mobile clicks off. EVELYN *looks at it.*

EVELYN *puts the mobile back in* JACKIE's *bag.*

EVELYN *picks up* JACKIE's *photo. She looks at it. She rips it up into little pieces and lets the pieces fall to the floor.*

JACKIE *re-enters wiping her mouth.*

JACKIE *sees the pieces of her photo on the floor.*

Your phone rang.

JACKIE *rushes to her phone.*

I answered it.

JACKIE. You didn't?

EVELYN. I told him you were here.

JACKIE. Oh God.

JACKIE *dialing a number. Putting the phone to her ear.*

Pick up. Pick up. Pick up, Dan.

JACKIE *clicks the phone off, tries to phone again.*

Pick up, Dan. Pick up.

JACKIE *tries again.*

JACKIE*'s phone bleeps a message.* JACKIE *cuts off the call.*

JACKIE *stares at the message.*

You've got no idea.

(*Shouting at the top of her voice.*) Yes, I am the mother of Daniel Miller.

EVELYN *looks up to the ceiling* (*concerned*).

EVELYN *shuts the door.*

Here I am. But nobody wants to hear what I've got to say, do they?

(*Talking normally.*)

Yet, we've all bloody got to listen to you, you and your speeches.

You want the whole world to think that we've lost so much just 'cause your son's dead. What would the world have been like with him in it? It would have been the bloody same. He died – nothing happened.

JACKIE *starts picking up the fragments of her photograph.*

The world never ended. He was just one little person. People die every day.

In fact, how many people have died in the last fifteen years, Evelyn? My dad died. Jack died.

EVELYN *gently picks up some keys on the side.*

EVELYN. Who's Jack?

EVELYN *starts to move slowly to the front door. Trying to move without getting* JACKIE*'s attention.*

JACKIE. They weren't all over the bloody papers like your son was, though. What's so special about your son?

EVELYN. He was murdered!

JACKIE. He was gonna be great, wasn't he?

EVELYN *continues moving slowly, slowly.*

EVELYN. Yes, he was.

JACKIE. And live this perfect little life –

EVELYN. A big life and all of it.

JACKIE. He was fifteen. How'd you know what he was going to be?

EVELYN. I know my son.

JACKIE. Years we've had to look at the one perfect picture you decided to show the world.

Beat.

Did you know who he was.

EVELYN. I did know.

EVELYN *continues moving.*

JACKIE. Did you? What sort of a man would he have been?

EVELYN. The best.

JACKIE *putting the fragments of the picture into her bag.*

EVELYN *at the front door.*

JACKIE. Perfect? Not just in prison like the rest of your lot, then?

EVELYN *quickly locks the door, but it's not a secret.*

What you doing?

EVELYN (*whispering*). Shh!

JACKIE. What?

EVELYN. Can you hear that?

JACKIE. Hear what?

EVELYN. Jason's outside the door.

JACKIE. No he isn't.

EVELYN. Yes he is. You just called him down.

JACKIE. No I nev–

EVELYN. You just told him who you are. You shouted it out. You shouldn't have done that, Jackie.

He's a big lad now, much bigger than he was in that court room all those years ago. He's got fifteen years of anger and he's bulked up on it. I don't know what he'll do... Now he knows you're here.

JACKIE *looks at the door grabbing up her bag.*

Can you even begin to imagine what he might do to you, Jackie?

JACKIE *shivers.*

But if you tell the truth, when he tries to open that door, I could tell him to leave you alone. I'm the only one he listens to now.

Take the stand, Jackie.

JACKIE *shaking her head, reluctant.*

EVELYN *gets the books moves them closer to her.*

Take the stand.

JACKIE *stands on the books.*

Raise your right hand.

JACKIE *complies slowly.*

EVELYN *places her hand on the bible*.

Do you swear... on the life of your unborn grandchild –

JACKIE. No!

EVELYN. Do you swear on the life of your unborn grandchild to tell the truth, the whole truth and nothing but the truth or else?

Silence.

I'll open the door, Jackie.

JACKIE *looks at the door*.

I'll tell him to come in, shall I?

JACKIE.... I do.

EVELYN. On 10th November 2005 where were you?

JACKIE. At home.

EVELYN. And where was your son?

Silence.

On your unborn grandchild's life, Jackie, where was your son?

JACKIE (*quietly*). He wasn't with me...

EVELYN. Sorry? I don't think I heard you properly. What did you just say?

JACKIE (*louder*). He wasn't with me.

EVELYN *weak on her feet*.

EVELYN *has to hold something or sit*.

EVELYN. On the night that my son was murdered, you wasn't with your son?

JACKIE *shakes her head no*.

You lied?

JACKIE. He... wasn't guilty of murdering your son.

EVELYN. How could you lie?

JACKIE *directs* EVELYN *to lower her voice.*

JACKIE. Shh…

Because you and your people were on a mission to frame –

EVELYN. To frame?

JACKIE. To frame my son and those… poor boys.

EVELYN. You lied?

JACKIE. I lied, but that didn't make Dan guilty of murdering your son.

EVELYN. The court relied on what you said. If he was at home with you, when you said he was, there was no way he could have killed my son!

JACKIE. There was no evidence to say he killed your son.

EVELYN. There was.

JACKIE.…That Hassan boy? Please.

Scoffs.

He lied. Our defence proved it. He lied.

EVELYN. He never lied.

JACKIE. As good as.

EVELYN. He picked them out.

JACKIE. Fingered our boys and couldn't tell his arse from his hand.

How d'you know it wasn't him or one of your lot that killed Michael. Because your lot kill each other all the time, don't they?

EVELYN *slaps* JACKIE *hard across the face.*

A stunned JACKIE *holds her left cheek.*

Beat.

EVELYN.... Where was Daniel? What was he doing?

JACKIE (*still holding her cheek*). He was out.

EVELYN. Out where?

JACKIE. Does it matter?

EVELYN. Of course it matters. Who was he with?

JACKIE. He did not kill your son.

EVELYN. They say the apple doesn't fall too far from the tree. And my God.

JACKIE. He... didn't kill your son.

EVELYN. I hate you. Everything that you are is written in your son's act. I can't tell you how much you disgust me.

JACKIE. Dan never had it in him. Did you see the little boy in the picture? Tell me that he had it in him to kill your son?

EVELYN. Let's say he was that perfect little blond-haired blue- eyed boy in that picture.

JACKIE. He was.

EVELYN. Then my God what did you do?

JACKIE. He couldn't of killed your son.

EVELYN. To turn that 'perfect little boy' into the murdering evil monster he is.

JACKIE. He's no monster.

EVELYN. You are the root, the most dangerous part. You are the part we don't see. The part that comes before. He's a symptom and you're the disease. I feel sorry for him having a mother like you.

JACKIE. What would you have done to save your son, Evelyn?

Beat.

If you had your time again and Michael is standing right here now. What would you do to save his life?

Beat.

Everything. Anything. Lie! Even if it weren't possible you'd do it. I lied to save his life from you. Because he said he didn't do it and lot you were making it look like he did.

EVELYN. How'd you know your son didn't kill mine?

JACKIE. Because I knew my son.

EVELYN. Ha.

JACKIE. I made him look me in the eye.

EVELYN. The same lying eyes as yours?

JACKIE. I made him tell me that he didn't do it... And he looked me in the eye and he told me that he didn't kill your son, and... I'm his mother.

EVELYN. And that was enough?

Beat.

JACKIE.... I'm sorry, Evelyn.

The women stare at each other.

I won't admit what I've just –

The thumping starts up again.

JACKIE *looks up to the ceiling.*

...If your son's outside this door, how can he be banging on the ceiling?

Beat.

You said –

EVELYN. I lied. He doesn't come down now, Jackie. Do you know why that is?

Beat.

Why don't you go up and have a look?

Beat.

See what you and your son and those boys and people like you have done to him...

EVELYN *opens the door and goes out.*

The sound of feet going slowly up the stairs.

JACKIE *uncertain.*

A beat.

EVELYN *comes back down with a wrapped birthday present.*

EVELYN *placing the present reverently on the sofa.*

JACKIE. What's that?

EVELYN *takes a breath. Begins to unwrap it.*

What you doing?

EVELYN *looks at* JACKIE *for a moment before continuing to unwrap the present.*

EVELYN *stares at the unwrapped present.*

JACKIE *goes over to see what the present is.*

EVELYN. He begged me for this. His old one, the basic one, broke, but all his friends had this one. I said 'I'll get you a new fancy phone when you get a job that can pay for it.' The day of his birthday I held it back. I gave him the books first. I wanted the phone to be a surprise. But he was so ungrateful. I held it back. He wouldn't get it until he apologised. He said... he wished I wasn't his mum.

Do you see what I'm left with?

Beat.

I'd do anything, just to know the truth, Jackie.

JACKIE*'s mobile phone rings.* JACKIE *looks at it. She lets it ring.*

EVELYN *goes to the front door and unlocks it.*

You'll want to answer that, it will be your son.

JACKIE *lets the phone ring.*

The phone stops.

JACKIE *sits down.*

JACKIE. Would you not give your speech?

EVELYN. What?

JACKIE. You said you'd do anything. For the truth. Well,
would you let it all go? Would you not give your speech,
never mention my son's name again? Squash any new
developments?

EVELYN. Do you know what you're asking?

JACKIE. But imagine knowing the truth, Evelyn. Imagine the
weight of all that lifted off of you.

EVELYN *thinks.*

EVELYN *shakes her head.*

Beat.

Imagine knowing, Evelyn.

EVELYN *shaking her head.*

EVELYN. No...

JACKIE. It's your decision, then.

JACKIE *gathers her things to go. Goes to the door touches
the door knob.*

EVELYN. Wait.

JACKIE. What?

Beat.

EVELYN *gives a nod.*

You get your bible then and you promise on your son's life.

JACKIE *locates the bible on the table. Gives it to* EVELYN.

Promise, on your son's life that what I'm about to say stays in
this room. That whatever happens, Dan is left completely out
of it. You don't keep coming for him, you leave us well alone.

Beat.

EVELYN....

JACKIE. Evelyn?

EVELYN. I, I promise.

JACKIE. On the one upstairs, his life.

Beat.

EVELYN.... I promise.

JACKIE puts her things down.

JACKIE. Then, Michael's in the park.

EVELYN. What?

JACKIE. You must have thought about it, played it out in your mind. God knows I have...

Beat.

Michael's in the park and it's dark. Why was he in the park? I thought he was going to his friend's.

EVELYN. This is how...? He's in the park...

...He's in the park... because I told him not to go to his dad's.

JACKIE. What's his dad got to do with it?

EVELYN. He thinks his dad has got him the phone. He's taking short cuts to get to his dad's.

JACKIE. Is that why you don't talk to your ex? Because you blame him?

Silence.

Oh no, Evelyn. You've got that wrong. Michael's been out since four. He wasn't going to his dad's. What's he been doing since four?

Beat.

Think, Evelyn.

Beat.

He didn't meet friends. He didn't go to the library.

EVELYN. He went to the library.

JACKIE. No he never. What was he doing?

Beat.

Was he with a girl?

EVELYN. No. Definitely not.

JACKIE. He probably was.

Beat.

Was she a white girl?

EVELYN. No. That can't be right. There'd have been…

JACKIE. DNA?

Evelyn.…Oh my God…

Beat.

Where is Daniel?

JACKIE. He was in the park earlier, but he's not in the park now. Not when it's dark.

EVELYN. You're sure?

JACKIE. Yeah. But I bet there's others in the park. And they're looking for little Sarah.

EVELYN. Who?

JACKIE.…Little Sarah Gibbs.

EVELYN. Sarah… Gibbs?

Beat.

…Oh my God.

JACKIE. That's right. There's a rumour. Little Sarah's in the park holding hands with that boy that they had a fight with earlier. They've been spotted.

EVELYN. Spotted by who?

JACKIE. Well, it's gotta be by her brothers hasn't it? Jimmy and Titch –

EVELYN. Titch?

JACKIE. Lewis Gibbs. They called him Titch 'cause he was little. And Titch wouldn't have gone without Jimmy. And Jimmy and Titch can't have their little step-sister copping off with a boy.

EVELYN. So, you are saying the two of them have gone out to look for my Michael and this Sarah?

JACKIE. That's right. They've been spotted and followed but when the boys get down to the ponds...

Beat.

JACKIE*'s tone changes.*

...they see Michael forcing himself onto her.

EVELYN. No they don't!

JACKIE. Yes they do. And what did you expect them to do? One of them says, let's say it's Jimmy, he says. 'Please can you leave my sister alone.' But your Michael doesn't take kindly to being interrupted and he jumps up all aggressively and he's a big lad for his age and he pulls a knife out from under his shirt.

EVELYN. You're a liar.

JACKIE. And he says something like, 'If you don't go now I'll stab you.'

EVELYN. Michael would never say that.

JACKIE. And he goes to stab Titch.

EVELYN. No he doesn't.

JACKIE. But Jimmy stops him and the knife falls to the ground and Michael turns to Jimmy and says 'I'm gonna kill you.'

EVELYN. Michael doesn't talk like that.

JACKIE. And Jimmy picks up the knife and before he knows what's happened Michael has lunged towards him and he accidently gets stabbed…

Beat.

EVELYN *still for a long moment.*

EVELYN.… So you're saying it was the two brothers that killed my son, that's what you're saying?

JACKIE. I'm saying that it was an accident. It was never meant to happen.

EVELYN. And that's what you, all of you – them boys and you and their families – told yourselves was the truth…? You all 'knew' this? You all sat there like butter wouldn't melt. Like you had nothing to do with it?

JACKIE. Who'd of believed our boys against yours, Evelyn? Everything's stacked against us, isn't it? As soon as the victim turned out to be black…

EVELYN. Turned out to be?

JACKIE. D'you think they'd have walked out the court room if the truth had been told? Course bloody not… It was just an accident, Evelyn, nothing more.

Beat.

That's the truth, Evelyn…

JACKIE *looking at her hands. Rubbing at them.*

Beat.

EVELYN. No. No… No. The only truth here is that you believe he deserved to die.

JACKIE *looks away.*

EVELYN *shaking her head.*

What about the other fourteen times he was stabbed! Did he lunge another fourteen times into the knife?

That's not what happened, Jackie, and you know it. In your
heart you know it.

EVELYN *directs* JACKIE *to the picture of* MICHAEL.

Look.

JACKIE *tries to avoid it.*

EVELYN *pulls* JACKIE *to the picture.*

He wasn't capable of what you accuse him of. Look at him.
Really look AT HIM.

JACKIE *finds it hard to look at the picture of* MICHAEL.

This is how I see it was.

JACKIE. It can't have been any other way, Evelyn.

EVELYN. It must have been another way. This is how I see it.
Michael's walking by himself on the path, his head down, his
hands in his pockets, minding his own business, when, okay,
this 'girl', 'Sarah', brushes past him. They were just walking
in the same direction, but not together.

JACKIE. Not together?

EVELYN. No. But those brothers and others, there must have
been others, misunderstood what they saw. They wasn't
holding hands. She just brushed past him.

JACKIE. Why would you kill someone for that?

EVELYN. Because he's black. That's why they're jeering him,
asking Michael where his tail is. 'Where's your banana. Go
back to where you come from.'

JACKIE. Maybe they don't say that.

EVELYN. Maybe, they do. He was in the park minding his own
business and he was set upon by a pack of racist wolves.
They brought a knife and they came looking for blood. His
blood.

JACKIE. That doesn't make sense, I think he left the path.

EVELYN. Why would he leave the path?

JACKIE. Because of Sarah. Sarah changes everything, Evelyn.

Beat.

A long time for EVELYN *to get her head around and to contemplate.*

JACKIE *thinking too.*

EVELYN.... So, let's say, for argument's sake, Michael is in the park... with a girl.

JACKIE. Sarah.

EVELYN. And let's say that there's a rumour.

JACKIE. That Sarah's in the park holding hands with a black boy. And Jimmy and Titch can't have their little sister copping off with a...

EVELYN. Nigga.

JACKIE *flinches.*

There must have been others.

JACKIE. I think it was just the two of them.

EVELYN. And you know that for a fact?

JACKIE. No. I don't know anything for a fact. But it makes sense for it to have been only the two brothers.

EVELYN. But boys like that don't hang out in twos, Jackie. They hang out in gangs. It must have been at least four.

JACKIE *thinks.*

JACKIE.... Well, okay four.

EVELYN. But Daniel's not one of the four?

JACKIE *shakes her head.*

JACKIE. No way. Definitely not.

Beat.

They've all had a bit to drink. Maybe a couple of spliffs and they're looking for something to do, now. They're bored.

EVELYN. They're bored?

JACKIE. None of them work, Evelyn. They've got nothing to look forward to. No prospects, no money. They sit around all day drinking cheap alcohol and puffing the odd spliff. They're at the bottom of the pile...

Beat.

Does Michael like this girl, Sarah, or is he just using her?

EVELYN. I don't know. Does it matter?

JACKIE. Evelyn, come on.

EVELYN. He's using her. She's a bike. Everyone's had her.

JACKIE. That's a bit strong. But you can understand why those lads were so miffed, can't you? Michael and Little Sarah deep into the park, round by the ponds where no one can see them and your Michael doesn't give a fig about her, not really – but it's all those lads' reputations on the line and in their little heads that's everything.

The four of them creep up. When they're almost on top of 'em one goes: 'Oi, oi!' What do they say next?

EVELYN. 'What are you doing here then?'

JACKIE. They're not coppers. They might say 'Keep on. Don't stop on account of us.' And Jimmy, the older one, hits Sarah hard across the face. 'Dirty, cock-sucking whore,' he says. Dashes her to the ground as she's pulling up her knickers and the six of them have surrounded him.

EVELYN. Six?

JACKIE.... Four.

Beat.

Michael is surrounded.

EVELYN. I want to say run.

JACKIE. Say it then.

EVELYN. 'Run! Run for your life, Michael... Run.'

JACKIE. But what's he doing?

EVELYN. He's trying to get to the girl, Sarah.

JACKIE. But they're pushing him away. What's he doing now?

EVELYN. Holding his ground. Standing tall, like I've taught
him. 'Don't let them bully boys see any weakness in you
Mikey. Stand your ground. Don't give an inch. They're all
watching you and you represent me.' But –

JACKIE. But, this Blackie in front of them is not running, he's
not scared. He's not giving an inch.

EVELYN. 'Don't we scare you, Nignog? You should be scared
of us'... He's starting to get scared now though.

JACKIE. Why?

EVELYN. Because one of them... Titch, has got a bottle. He's
waving it around.

JACKIE. Good that's the bottle. Then one of them gets a smart
idea. He turns to Sarah, who's on the floor holding her cheek
and says: 'Did he force himself onto you, Sar? Did this big
"Blackie" rape you?'

EVELYN. No...

JACKIE. Yes, and Little Sarah fears them and her dad (you
know who her dad is don't you?) much more than she cares
for your son. And so she says:

EVELYN. '...He did.'

JACKIE. 'Yeah. He did. Pushed me back here where no one
could see us. Dragged me into these bushes and forced
himself on me.'

EVELYN. 'He beat me up. Look at what he did to my face. I'm
bleeding?...'

JACKIE. And suddenly Michael's bricking it. Because...

EVELYN. Rape…? That's serious and it's… her word against his.

JACKIE. And don't forget who her dad is… And Michael's just had sex with her…

EVELYN. Maybe he didn't.

JACKIE. Or maybe he did.

EVELYN. He's thinking, 'No one's going to believe me. That's my whole life. Finished.'

JACKIE.…And his mum's gonna kill him.

EVELYN. I'm not going to kill you, baby… I don't care what you've done or not done. Walk away. Please… Walk away, right now…

Beat.

What are they doing?

JACKIE. They're calling him a dirty black rapist bastard, Evelyn.

Beat.

They've dropped the bottle.

Beat.

They're walking away.

EVELYN. They can't be walking away?

JACKIE. They're walking away and they're laughing too. Titch says, nice and loud, 'When we get home, Sar, you call Dad and tell him what's happened. Then Dad'll call Uncle Bobbie and you know what they do to dirty raping black bastards down at the station, don't you?'

EVELYN. He's only fifteen. He's just a baby…

JACKIE. And then Michael picks up the bottle.

EVELYN. No he doesn't.

JACKIE. You know he does, Evelyn. He picks it up and smashes it on the floor.

EVELYN. Michael, don't!

JACKIE. Michael shouts, what does he shout, Evelyn?

EVELYN (*with everything she's got*). 'You racist cunts!'

A long beat.

What happens next?

Silence.

Jackie?

Silence.

They're all turning back, aren't they?

Maybe, one of them, Titch, he says to Michael, 'What did you call us?'

The hatred and menace is written all over their faces. They've got no mercy.

They can smell his blood.

They want to spill my innocent baby's blood.

They remember the fight from earlier, how Michael must have shown them up, stood his ground. He must of made them feel so small. So they went home didn't they? Got themselves tooled up because he needed to be taught a lesson didn't he? A lesson he would never forget. And they decided long before they got into that park that they were going to butcher him, that they were going to end his life.

And Michael doesn't see the knife.

Beat.

Where's the knife, Jackie?

Beat.

Jackie? Where's the knife?

JACKIE.…Oh God!

EVELYN. Jackie?

JACKIE. No. We've got to stop.

EVELYN. We can't stop.

Silence.

D'you think Michael was allowed to stop?

Silence.

Can you imagine the pain, Jackie? The pain they brought to his body, again and again and again and again as they cut him down.

We cannot stop.

JACKIE *looking up at* MICHAEL*'s picture.*

Jackie!

Where's the knife?

Beat.

Where's the knife, Jackie!

JACKIE.…Tucked into one of their trousers.

EVELYN. Whose trousers?

Silence.

Jackie?

Silence.

Jackie…

JACKIE. It's… It's got to be Dan's.

A long beat.

EVELYN. But you said… Daniel wasn't there.

JACKIE. He was there…

Fifteen times. That's not an accident. That's not self-defence. That's cold blooded…

EVELYN. Murder…

JACKIE.…It's the knife…

Beat.

EVELYN. They never found the knife.

JACKIE. They never did find the knife but it's the knife.

EVELYN. What are you talking about?

Beat.

JACKIE. Dad kept all Dan's trophies… He never kept anyone elses.' All of them trophies and every single one of them belongs to Dan.

JACKIE *is looking at her hands.*

Six inches. I always thought it was bigger. Wooden handle with little curves where your fingers sit to make the handle more comfortable. The grip more certain. It doesn't have to be that knife, could be any knife, but why else would he have kept it with Dan's trophies?

He was so proud of his boy…

I swear to you, Evelyn, I never thought not once that Dan could do that. Not really. Not really… I thought, okay, he might of been there (and he was a damned silly bugger for being there!), but he wasn't directly involved. Can you understand, that that makes all the difference, Evelyn? And that is what he said – It was an accident and it was the brothers, no way was it him. So I always was just protecting my innocent little boy. But then. I'm going through Dad's stuff. He's got so much stuff but then I find a knife and…

EVELYN. You've got the knife?

JACKIE.…It can't be I'm thinking. It's too small. That knife was bigger. And Dan tells me, 'Don't be silly, Mum, that's not the knife. That knife's too small. The knife was bigger.' And I want to believe him so badly because…

I can't breathe.

EVELYN *rushes out. We hear the rush of the tap then she returns with a glass of water and hands it to* JACKIE.

A beat as JACKIE *looks at it. Then drinks from it.*

What does that make him, Evelyn?

What does that make me?

EVELYN....And you said six.

JACKIE. I know it won't make sense to you now... but I've hated the person who dobbed in our boys. Coward. Called up from a telephone box after

EVELYN....seeing my appeal.

JACKIE....and gave the names of our four boys. I racked my brains – who could have done something so... Drew a blank. But as I'm thinking about it now, Jack Marsdon, sitting at my table, keeps popping into my head.

EVELYN. Jack Marsdon?

JACKIE. And wherever Jack was Alfie was.

EVELYN. Alfie?

JACKIE....Marsdon. Cousins. They was around the older boys like flies. Sometimes the whole ruddy lot of them would be at mine for their tea, at my table. Not enough chairs Jack would be on the floor. A lovely boy was Jack. Bit more sensitive than the others though...

Beat.

There was something funny when he died.

EVELYN. How did he die?

JACKIE....Hanged himself.

Beat.

There was something funny when he died with the parents. Couldn't put my finger on it at the time but I suppose, it was a bit embarrassed... And my dad, dismissive. 'Kids like that don't deserve tears...'As if...

Beat.

EVELYN. It was Jack in the phone box. It... was... Jack... in the phone box.

JACKIE. Must of been. Must have saw you on the TV again, months after and decided couldn't live with himself. The two younger ones was probably there but not really there and Jack couldn't have grassed up his own cousin... because

(*Puts on her dad's husky voice.*) 'You don't grass up your own do you?'

(*Back to normal voice.*) You was right about the seeds...

It was always the same joke...

Beat.

(*Puts on her dad's husky voice.*) 'A black fella walks into a bar with a parrot on his shoulder...

The barman says "That's unusual. Where'd' you get it from?"

"In the jungle."

Beat.

"There's millions of em." Says the parrot.

Beat.

JACKIE *and* EVELYN *frozen.*

A long beat.

JACKIE*'s mobile starts to ring.*

Both women look at the phone.

The phone rings off.

A few seconds later JACKIE*'s phone bleeps a message.*

JACKIE *locates her phone and looks at the message.*

A beat.

JACKIE *gets active. Wipes her face. Tidies herself up.*

EVELYN *goes over to a house phone. Dials.*

JACKIE *goes over to* EVELYN. *Holds her arm.*

Beat.

EVELYN. You do it.

EVELYN *hands the phone receiver to* JACKIE. *But it sits in mid air for a long beat.*

JACKIE *hangs her head.*

JACKIE (*shaking her head*). I can't.

EVELYN *shakes her head.*

I'm only what I am, Evelyn. I'm not strong like you.

Beat.

It's my grandchild. That's all I've got, now.

EVELYN *shakes her head, starts dialling.*

JACKIE *touches* EVELYN*'s arm again.* EVELYN *looks to where* JACKIE*'s hand is touching her arm.*

EVELYN. You can't possibly expect me to be tied by that promise, not now.

Beat.

JACKIE. There's something else you should know first.

EVELYN *holds the phone.*

Things aren't always what they seem. They aren't always black and white.

Beat.

Sometimes, there's stuff in the middle.

EVELYN. You said the 'stuff' in the middle we should ignore. That the stuff in the middle were the mistakes.

JACKIE. I was wrong.

EVELYN *dialling.*

It's about Sarah.

EVELYN *lowers the phone but still holds the receiver.*

EVELYN. Sarah?

The thumping from upstairs starts up again.

JACKIE.…Just after… the murder… Sarah's mum sends her away. Up north. Manchester I think… There are loads of rumours flying around. We all knew… thought we knew what had happened to that poor girl – you know, rape – but yet the mum keeps saying as far as she is concerned Little Sarah is dead… well that's harsh ain't it? Why would you say that about your own daughter?

Beat.

So with her saying that, the rumour that I believe, the one that makes most sense to me, is the one that said Little Sarah was pregnant.

EVELYN.…Pregnant?

JACKIE.…and wouldn't get rid of the baby…

Beat.

Things aren't always black and white, Evelyn…sometimes… all you've got to hold onto, is the mistakes.

JACKIE *gathers her things to go.*

EVELYN, *still with the phone in her hand, watches* JACKIE *leave.*

The End.

A Nick Hern Book

seeds first published in Great Britain as a paperback original in 2020 by Nick Hern Books Limited, The Glasshouse, 49a Goldhawk Road, London W12 8QP

seeds copyright © 2020 Mel Pennant

Mel Pennant has asserted her right to be identified as the author of this work

Cover photograph by Wasi Daniju

Designed and typeset by Nick Hern Books, London
Printed in Great Britain by Mimeo Ltd, Huntingdon, Cambridgeshire PE29 6XX

A CIP catalogue record for this book is available from the British Library

ISBN 978 1 84842 945 1

Woodland CARBON
www.woodlandcarbon.co.uk
NICK HERN BOOKS
Printed on Carbon Captured paper

www.nickhernbooks.co.uk

facebook.com/nickhernbooks

twitter.com/nickhernbooks